Written by HELEN SNYDER BENNETT

# JACK'S AMAZING MAGIC BED

Illustrated by MICHAEL J. HONE

*To Gordon & Kathleen*

HSB

*To my wife Lynne & Elizabeth A. Edelson*

MJH



Published by Tomac Publishing
P.O. Box 247
Old Greenwich, CT 06870

Designed by Mary Repetti, Guilford, CT
Printed by Van Dyck/Columbia, North Haven, CT

ISBN-0-9638747-0-5

Jack had been REALLY sick and had to have a funny-looking hospital bed put in his room at home.

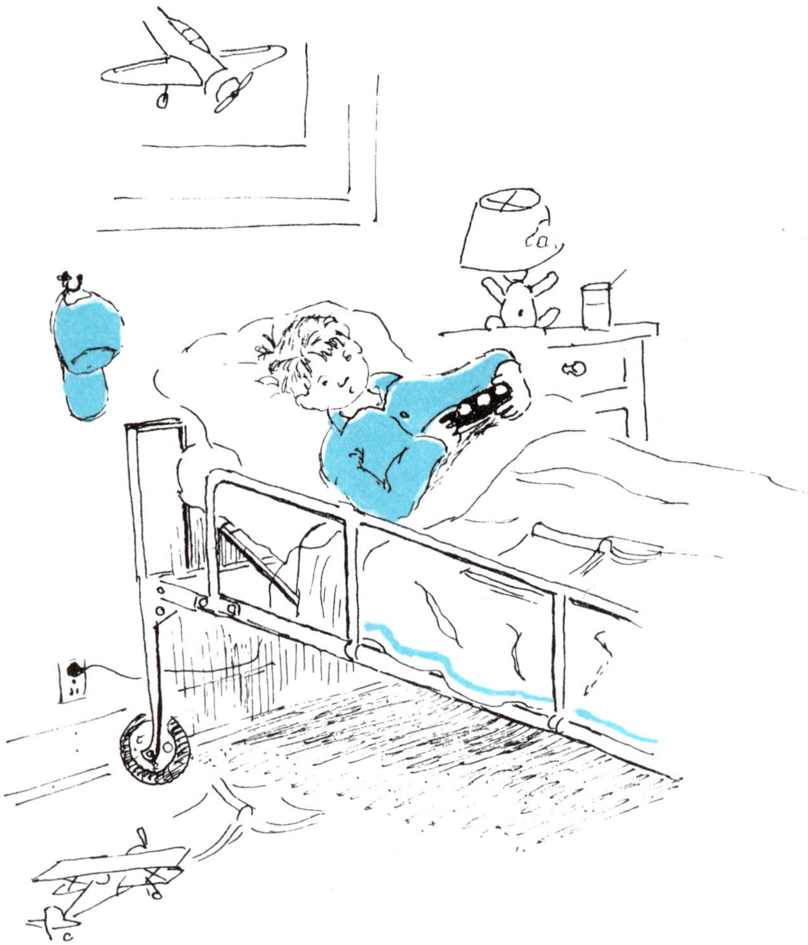

The bed had a control panel with three buttons. Jack could push one button to raise up the head, another one to raise the foot, and a third one to make the whole bed go up and down like an elevator. "Oh, boy," he thought, "this bed is fun."

One day Jack was in bed wishing he could go somewhere. "Well," he decided, "I'll just pretend my bed is a car and that I'm driving it on a trip!" So he started pushing all the control buttons. Suddenly, like magic, his bed began to roll on its wheels. "Wow!" he said to himself, "MAYBE I'VE GOT A MAGIC BED! I can even go into New York City, like I did once with my school."

Jack always loved going different places, but since he'd been sick and hadn't been riding his bike or going anywhere, he was a little scared to drive his magic bed out the front door. He thought, "I'd better stop and check my control buttons–which one makes the bed turn left, which makes it turn right, and which one makes it go straight ahead. OK, I'm ready." He turned his magic bed to the right and drove off down the street.

Finally, Jack was on the big highway where lots of cars and trucks were whizzing past his magic bed. But he wasn't sure he was going the right way. Then he remembered, "People say truck drivers know the best way to go." When the driver of a long, shiny truck waved, Jack felt, "I want to follow him."

Soon Jack saw a sign—GEORGE WASHINGTON BRIDGE. "Great!" But then he had a terrible thought. "To go over the bridge in my magic bed I'll have to pay money to the man in the toll booth. And I don't have ANY!"

"Oh, goodness," Jack muttered, "I bet I'll have to turn around and go back home." At first, the man looked cross. Then he smiled and said, "Well, I don't think people who drive magic beds have to pay. Have a good time."

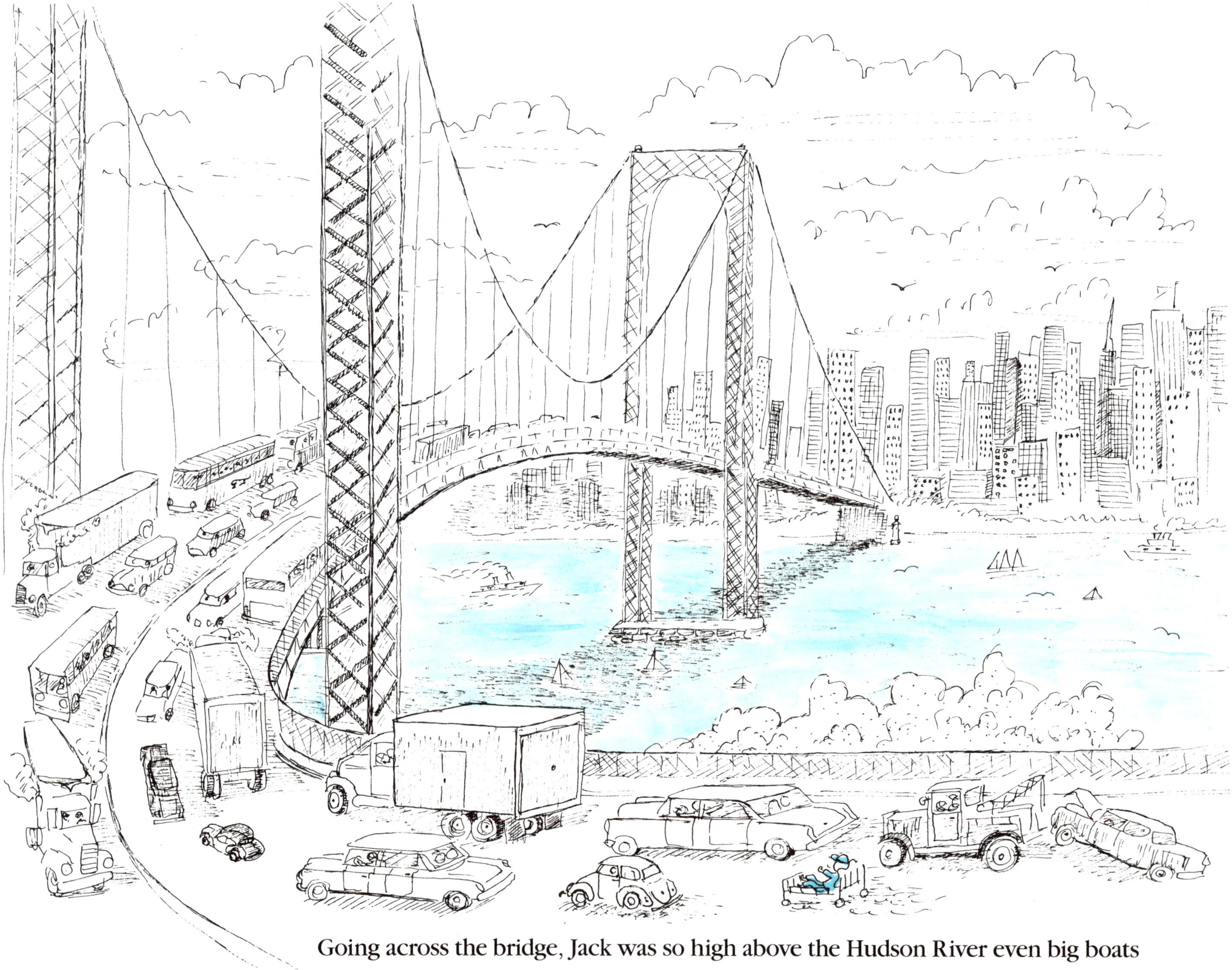

Going across the bridge, Jack was so high above the Hudson River even big boats looked small, and little sailboats looked like toys in the bathtub.

When he got off the bridge, Jack was really in New York City. "Whoopee! I made it!" he yelled. But he almost bounced out of his magic bed when a wheel hit a deep pothole, and from there on he drove more slowly on the wide, busy road beside the river.

Suddenly, Jack could not believe his eyes! Anchored at the dock was the highest, longest, most enormous ship he had ever seen in his life–the aircraft carrier INTREPID. It was as tall as a building!

From way up on the deck a man called down, "Hey, come on up." Jack shouted back, "I can't, because I can't get out of my bed yet." "OK," the man called back. "We'll come down and get you." Two really strong men picked Jack up in his magic bed as easy as pie, and put him into the elevator that brought airplanes up to the flight deck.

And there he was in his magic bed, on the huge flight deck. Jack was stunned. “Gosh! This deck is as long as three football fields!” There were great airplanes parked all around.

"Best of all," he told the men, "I like the long, pointy black one–it's called a Blackbird. And next time I'll bring a friend to see it. Now I have to go. Thanks a whole lot for carrying me up here."

Down on the street again, Jack was driving along looking at the river, when he heard a siren screaming. Tearing around the corner was the fire chief's car, coming right at him! Jack was so scared he almost fell out of his magic bed, but he pulled over to let the big hook and ladder truck go past. That was a close one.

Soon Jack saw the Twin Towers, the two most fantastically high skyscrapers in New York. "Gosh," he thought, "they really do look like they're scraping the sky!" To see the tops he had to lean way, way back in his magic bed.

Across the street was a park at the edge of the water, and Jack stopped to look at the beautiful Statue of Liberty standing on a little island far out in the harbor. But he felt a little sad. "Even if I could get out to the Statue on a ferry boat, I could never get my magic bed up inside to look out the windows in her crown. But," he added softly to himself, "SOMEDAY I'll be back WITHOUT my bed."

By now, Jack was tired and he wanted to go home. And a whole mob of other people wanted to get home, too. He wondered, “How can I EVER find my way back with these millions of cars?”

Driving along the East River, Jack could see a helicopter and pilot on a landing platform right next to the road. "Great!" he thought, "That pilot can tell me the way to get home." "Sure, kid," the pilot said, "but why don't I FLY you home?" So the pilot put some straps around the magic bed to attach it under his helicopter, then he and the co-pilot jumped in. "Remember, hold on tight," he told Jack. "We're ready to go."

For Jack, this was really DOUBLE MAGIC! "Want to fly past the Statue of Liberty?" the pilot called. "Wonderful!" Jack called back. And they swooped down so close to the Statue he could see people looking out the little windows in her crown! This was even better than going on a ferry boat.

“Now, where shall we go?” the pilot asked. “Oh, anywhere,” Jack said. “OK, we’ll give you a view of the whole city.” In a minute Jack called out, “You know what? Down there it looks like a great big jigsaw puzzle–apartment houses, offices, parks, stores and hotels and streets and parking lots and skyscrapers all fitted tight together! Awesome!”

"Next, we're going to fly across Central Park," the co-pilot called. Up ahead Jack could see a lot of trees and grass and people riding bicycles and horses pulling carriages full of tourists. He thought they must already be out in the country. But it was only the hugeness of Central Park. Then, he spotted the famous Metropolitan Museum. "Look!" Jack shouted, "There's the museum where I went with my class. We saw knights in armor and African masks and all kinds of good stuff."

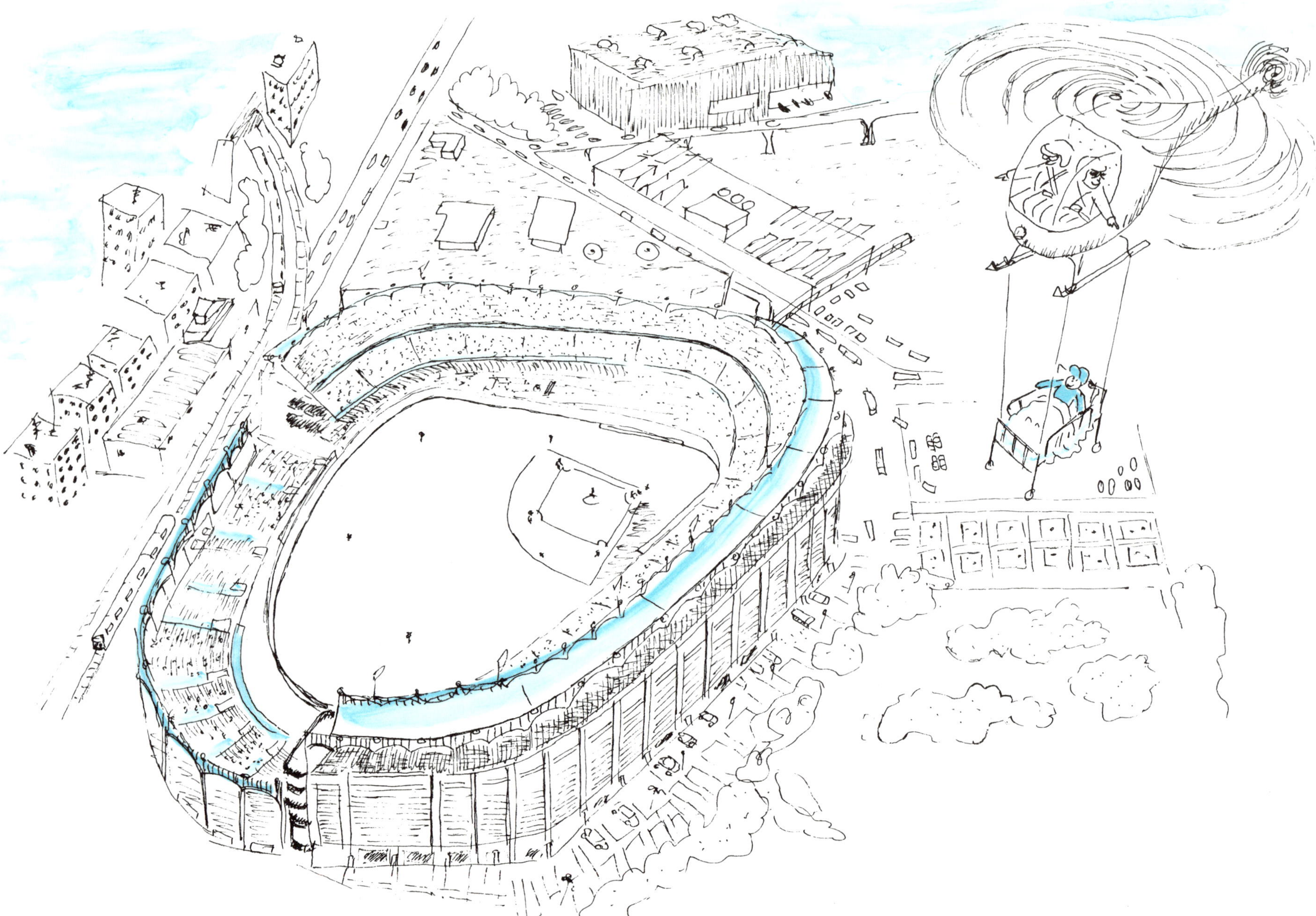

"Now, Jack," the pilot said, "I've got just a little more time before I have to get back. Where next?" "Well," Jack asked, "could we maybe fly over Yankee Stadium? So the pilot turned the helicopter, and Jack could look right down on the baseball diamond and even see tiny players. "Wouldn't it be fun to see a home run from up in the air?"

A few minutes later, the pilot said, “Now, we’re back across the Hudson River. Which way is your house?” Jack felt a lump in the middle of his stomach. “Oh,” he said in a shaky voice, “from up here I can’t tell which is the right road.” “Well, kid,” the pilot said, “you better look hard, or I’ll have to take you back to New York in your magic bed. Look out for some special building.”

Jack felt REALLY lost. He had NO idea where they were. From up in the air everything looked so different. Then he shouted, “Hey! There it is! There it is! Over there. The church with the tall steeple. And there’s my house! Across the street–the one with the blue car.”

“Looks like a good place to land,” the pilot said. “And, hey, Jack, some kids are watching us coming in for a landing!” Jack’s magic bed made a couple of bumps, then stopped on the grass, and the pilot untied the straps to his bed. “I’m sort of sorry to be down on the ground,” Jack said. “Flying through the air in my bed I felt like a bird. But thanks a million for the great ride.” “I was real glad to do it,” the pilot replied, “and it sure was fun to meet a magic bed driver.” Then he waved, “So long, Jack, hope I’ll see you again sometime.” The co-pilot waved, too, and they took off in their helicopter–straight up.

Jack drove back into his bedroom, and this time he parked himself where he could look out the window. He was very tired, but very happy, too. Before he fell asleep Jack thought, "Oh, boy! Even if I have to stay in bed a little while longer, I'm not scared to drive my magic bed off on another trip."

THIS BOOK BELONGS TO:

______________________________